A Journal of a Tour of Discovery Across the Blue Mountains, New South Wales in the year 1813

by

Gregory Blaxland

SYDNEY UNIVERSITY PRESS

SYDNEY UNIVERSITY PRESS
SETIS at the University of Sydney Library
University of Sydney
www.sup.usyd.edu.au

Originally published in Sydney by Gibbs, Shallard and Co. in 1870.

The publication of this book is part of the University of Sydney Library's
Australian Studies electronic texts initiative. Further details are available at
www.sup.usyd.edu.au/oztexts/

Sydney University Press
Fisher Library
University of Sydney
NSW Australia 2006

E-mail: info@sup.usyd.edu.au

ISBN 1 920897 48 8

For current information see http://purl.library.usyd.edu.au/sup/1920897488

Designed in Australia at the University Publishing Service
University of Sydney

Preface.

THE Journal of my father, giving an account of his passage over the Blue Mountains in 1813, and published in London in 1823, is no longer to be had. Frequent enquiries have been made for it; and recently I have discovered a stray copy. There is but one survivor of the expedition — W. C. WENTWORTH, Esq.; and in order to perpetuate the memory of the successful exploration of my father and his companions, I reprint his Journal, with his original dedication of it to his uncle.

JOHN BLAXLAND.
Ryde, January, 1870.

To John Oxley Parker, ESQ., of Chelmsford, Essex.

LONDON, FEBRUARY 10, 1823.

DEAR SIR, — Feelings of gratitude for your kind attention to me in the early part of life, have induced me to dedicate to you the following short Journal of my passage over the Blue Mountains, in the colony of New South Wales, under the persuasion that it will afford you pleasure at all times to hear that any of your family have been instrumental in promoting the prosperity of any country in which they may reside, however distant that country may be from the immediate seat of our Government.

Since my return to England many of my friends have expressed a wish to peruse my Journal. To meet their request in the only practicable or satisfactory manner, I have consented to its being printed. Devoid as it is of any higher pretensions than belong to it as a plain unvarnished statement, it may not be deemed wholly uninteresting, when it is is considered what important alterations the result of the expedition has produced in the immediate interests and prosperity of the colony. This appears in nothing more decidedly than the unlimited pasturage already afforded to the very fine flocks of merino sheep, as well as the extensive field opened for the exertions of the present, as well as future generations. It has changed the aspect of the colony, from a confined insulated tract of land, to a rich and extensive continent.

This expedition, which has proved so completely successful, resulted from two previous attempts. One of these was made by water, by His Excellency the Governor, in person, whom I accompanied. We ascended the River Hawkesbury, or Nepean, from above Emu Island, to the mouth of the Warragomby, or Great Western River, where it emerges from the mountains, and joins itself to that river, from its mouth. We proceeded as far as it was navigable by a small boat, which is only a few miles further. It was found to lose itself at different places, almost entirely underneath and between immense blocks of stones, being confined on each side by perpendicular cliffs of the same kind of stone, which sometimes rose as high as the tops of the mountains, through which it appears to have forced, or worn its way, with the assistance, probably, of an earthquake, or some other great convulsion of nature.

The other expedition was undertaken by myself, attended by three European servants and two natives, with a horse to carry provisions and other necessaries. We travelled on the left, or south bank of the western river, and found no impediment, by keeping in the cow pastures, and crossing the different streams of water before they enter the rocks and precipices close to the river. We were unable, however, to penetrate westward, finding ourselves turned eastward towards the coast. We returned sooner than I intended, owing to one man being taken ill. The natives proved but of little use, which determined me not to take them again on my more distant expedition, Very little information can be obtained from any tribe out of their own district, which is seldom more than about thirty miles square. This journey confirmed me in the opinion, that it was practicable to find a passage over the mountains, and I resolved at some future period to attempt it, by endeavoring to cross the river, and reach the high land on its northern bank by the ridge which appeared to run westward, between the Warragomby and the River Grose. I concluded, that if no more difficulties were found in travelling than had been experienced on the other side, we must be able to advance westward towards the interior of the country, and have a fair chance of passing the mountains. On inquiry, I found a person who had been accustomed to hunt the kangaroo in the mountains, in the direction I wished to go; who undertook to take the horses to the top of the first ridge. Soon after I mentioned the circumstance to His Excellency the Governor, who thought it reasonable, and expressed a wish that I should make the attempt. Having made every requisite preparation, I applied to the two gentlemen who accompanied me, to join in the expedition, and was fortunate in obtaining their consent. Before we set out, we laid down the plan to be pursued, and the course to be attempted, namely, to ascend the ridge before-mentioned, taking the streams of water on the left, which appeared to empty themselves into the Warragomby, as our guide; being careful not to cross any of them, but to go round their sources, so as to be certain of keeping between them and the streams that emptied themselves into the River Grose.

To these gentlemen I have to express my thanks for their company, and to acknowledge that without their assistance I should have had but little chance of success.

The road which has since been made deviates but a few rods in some places from the line cleared of the small trees and bushes and marked by us. Nor does it appear likely that any other line of road will ever be discovered than at the difficult and narrow passes that we were fortunate to discover; by improving which, a good carriage road has now been made across the mountains. Mount York is the western summit of the mountains; the Vale Clwyd the first valley at their foot; from which a mountain (afterwards named Mount Blaxland by His Excellency Governor Macquarie) is about eight miles, which terminated our journey.

I remain, dear Sir, most respectfully,
Your affectionate Nephew,
G. BLAXLAND.

A journal, &C.

ON Tuesday, May 11, 1813, Mr. Gregory Blaxland, Mr. William Wentworth, and Lieutenant Lawson, attended by four servants, with five dogs, and four horses laden with provisions, ammunition, and other necessaries, left Mr. Blaxland's farm at the South Creek, for the purpose of endeavoring to effect a passage over the Blue Mountains, between the Western River, and the River Grose. They crossed the Nepean, or Hawkesbury River, at the ford, on to Emu Island, at four o'clock p.m., and having proceeded, according to their calculation, two miles in a south-west direction, through forest land and good pasture, encamped at five o'clock at the foot of the first ridge. The distance travelled on this and on the subsequent days was computed by time, the rate being estimated at about two miles per hour. Thus far they were accompanied by two other gentlemen.

On the following morning (May 12), as soon as the heavy dew was off, which was about nine a.m., they proceeded to ascend the ridge at the foot of which they had camped the preceding evening. Here they found a large lagoon of good water, full of very coarse rushes. The high land of Grose Head appeared before them at about seven miles distance, bearing north by east. They proceeded this day about three miles and a quarter, in a direction varying from south-west to west-north-west; but, for a third of the way, due west. The land was covered with scrubby brush-wood, very thick in places, with some trees of ordinary timber, which much incommoded the horses. The greater part of the way they had deep rocky gullies on each side of their track, and the ridge they followed was very crooked and intricate. In the evening they encamped at the head of a deep gully, which they had to descend for water; they found but just enough for the night, contained in a hole in the rock, near which they met with a kangaroo, who had just been killed by an eagle. A small patch of grass supplied the horses for the night.

They found it impossible to travel through the brush before the dew was off, and could not, therefore, proceed at an earlier hour in the morning than nine. After travelling about a mile on the third day, in a west and north-west direction, they arrived at a large tract of forest land, rather hilly, the grass and timber tolerably good, extending, as they imagine, nearly to Grose Head, in the same direction nearly as the river. They computed it at two thousand acres. Here they found a track marked by a European, by cutting the bark of the trees. Several native huts presented themselves at different places. They had not proceeded above two miles, when they found themselves stopped by a brush-wood much thicker than they had hitherto met with. This induced them to alter their course, and to endeavor to find another passage to the westward; but every ridge which they explored proved to terminate in a deep rocky precipice; and they had no alternative but to return to the thick brushwood, which appeared to be the main ridge, with the determination to cut a way through for the horses next day. This day some of the horses, while standing, fell several times under their loads. The dogs killed a large kangaroo. The party encamped in the forest tract, with plenty of good grass and water.

On the next morning, leaving two men to take care of the horses and provisions, they proceeded to cut a path through the thick brushwood, on what they considered as the main ridge of the mountain, between the Western River and the River Grose; keeping the heads of the gullies, which were supposed to empty themselves into the Western River on their left hand, and into the River Grose on their right. As they ascended the mountain these gullies became much deeper and more rocky on each side. They now began to mark their track by cutting the bark of the trees on two sides. Having cut their way for about five miles, they returned in the evening to the spot on which they had encamped the night before. The fifth day was spent in prosecuting the same tedious operation; but, as much time was necessarily lost in walking twice over the track cleared the day before, they were unable to cut away more than two miles further. They found no food for the horses the whole way. An emu was heard on the other side of the gulley, calling continually in the night.

On Sunday they rested, and arranged their future plan. They had reason, however, to regret this suspension of their proceedings, as it gave the men leisure to ruminate on their danger; and it was for some time doubtful whether, on the next day, they could be persuaded to venture farther. The dogs this day killed two small kangaroos. They barked and ran off continually during the whole night; and at day-light, a most tremendous howling of native dogs was heard, who appeared to have been watching them during the night.

On Monday, the 17th, having laden the horses with as much grass as could be put on them, in addition to their other burdens, they moved forward along the path which they had cleared and marked, about six miles and a half. The bearing of the route they had been obliged to keep along the ridge, varied exceedingly; it ran sometimes in a north-north-western direction — sometimes south-east, or due south, but generally south-west, or south-south-west. They encamped in the afternoon between two very deep gulleys, on a narrow bridge, Grose Head bearing north-east by north; and Mount Banks north-west by west. They had to fetch water up the side of the precipice, about six hundred feet high, and could get scarcely enough for the party. The horses had none this night; they performed their journey well, not having to stand under their loads.

The following day was spent in cutting a passage through the brushwood, for a mile and a half further. They returned to their camp at five o'clock, very much tired and dispirited. The ridge, which was not more than fifteen or twenty yards over, with deep precipices on each side, was rendered almost impassable by a perpendicular mass of rock, nearly thirty feet high, extending across the whole breadth, with the exception of a small broken rugged track in the centre. By removing a few large stones, they were enabled to pass.

On Wednesday, the 19th, the party moved forward along this path; bearing chiefly west, and west-south-east. They now began to ascend the second ridge of the mountains, and from this elevation they obtained for the first time an extensive view of the settlements below. Mount Banks bore north-west; Grose Head, north-east; Prospect Hill, east by south; the Seven Hills, east-north-east;

6

Windsor, north-east by east. At a little distance from the spot at which they began the ascent, they found a pyramidical heap of stones, the work, evidently, of some European, one side of which the natives had opened, probably in the expectation of finding some treasure deposited in it. This pile they concluded to be the one erected by Mr. Bass, to mark the end of his journey. That gentleman attempted, some time ago, to pass the mountains, and to penetrate into the interior; but having got thus far, he gave up the undertaking as impracticable; reporting, on his return, that it was impossible to find a passage even for a person on foot. Here, therefore, the party had the satisfaction of believing that they had penetrated as far as any European had been before them.

They encamped this day to refresh their horses, at the head of a swamp covered with a coarse rushy grass, with a small run of good water through the middle of it. In the afternoon, they left their camp to mark and cut a road for the next day.

They proceeded with the horses on the 20th nearly five miles, and encamped at noon at the head of a swamp about three acres in extent, covered with the same coarse rushy grass as the last station, with a stream of water running through it. The horses were obliged to feed on the swamp grass, as nothing better could be found for them. The travellers left the camp as before, in the afternoon, to cut a road for the morrow's journey. The ridge along which their course lay now became wider and more rocky, but was still covered with brush and small crooked timber, except at the heads of the different streams of water which ran down the side of the mountain, where the land was swampy and clear of trees. The track of scarcely any animal was to be seen, and very few birds. One man was here taken dangerously ill with a cold. Bearing of the route at first, south-westerly; afterwards north-north-west, and west-north-west.

Their progress the next day was nearly four miles, in a direction still varying from north-west-by-north to south-west. They encamped in the middle of the day at the head of a well-watered swamp, about five acres in extent; pursuing, as before, their operations in the afternoon. In the beginning of the night the dogs ran off and barked violently. At the same time something was distinctly heard to run through the brushwood, which they supposed to be one of the horses got loose; but they had reason to believe afterwards that they had been in great danger — that the natives had followed their track, and advanced on them in the night, intending to have speared them by the light of their fire, but that the dogs drove them off.

On Saturday, the 22nd instant, they proceeded in the track marked the preceding day rather more than three miles, in a south-westerly direction, when they reached the summit of the third and highest ridge of the mountains southward of Mount Banks. From the bearing of Prospect Hill and Grose Head, they computed this spot to be eighteen miles in a straight line from the River Nepean, at the point at which they crossed it. On the top of this ridge they found about two thousand acres of land clear of trees, covered with loose stones and short coarse grass, such as grows on some of the commons in England. Over this heath they proceeded for about a mile and a half, in a south-westerly direction, and encamped by the side of a fine stream of water, with just wood enough on the banks to serve for firewood. From the summit they had a fine view of all the settlements and country eastward, and of a great extent of country to the westward and south-west. But their progress in both the latter directions was stopped by an impassable barrier of rock, which appeared to divide the interior from the coast as with a stone wall, rising perpendicularly out of the side of the mountain.

In the afternoon they left their little camp in the charge of three of the men, and made an attempt to descend the precipice by following some of the streams of water, or by getting down at some of the projecting points where the rocks had fallen in; but they were baffled in every instance. In some places the perpendicular height of the rocks above the earth below could not be less than four hundred feet. Could they have accomplished a descent, they hoped to procure mineral specimens which might throw light on the geological character of the country, as the strata appeared to be exposed for many hundred feet, from the top of the rock to the beds of the several rivers beneath. The broken rocky country on the western side of the cow pasture has the appearance of having acquired its present form from an earthquake, or some other dreadful convulsion of nature, at a much later period than the mountains northward, of which Mount Banks forms the southern extremity. The aspect of the country which lay beneath them much disappointed the travellers: it appeared to consist of sand and small scrubby brushwood, intersected with broken rocky mountains, with streams of water running between them to the eastward, towards one point, where they probably form the Western River, and enter the mountains.

They now flattered themselves that they had surmounted half the difficulties of their undertaking, expecting to find a passage down the mountain more to the northward.

On the next day they proceeded about three miles and a half; but the trouble occasioned by the horses when they got off the open land induced them to recur to their former plan of devoting the afternoon to marking and clearing a tract for the ensuing day, as the most expeditious method of proceeding, notwithstanding that they had to go twice over the same ground. The bearing of their course this day was, at first, north-east and north, and then changed to north-west and north-north-west. They encamped on the side of a swamp, with a beautiful stream of water running through it.

Their progress on the next day was four miles and a-half, in a direction varying from north-north-west to south-south-west: they encamped, as before, at the head of a swamp. This day, between ten and eleven a.m., they obtained a sight of the country below, when the clouds ascended. As they were marking a road for the morrow, they heard a native chopping wood very near them, who fled at the approach of the dogs.

On Tuesday, the 25th, they could proceed only three miles and a-half in a varying direction, encamping at two o'clock at the side of a swamp. The underwood being very prickly and full of small thorns, annoyed them very much. This day they saw the track of the woombat* for the first time. On the 26th they proceeded two miles and three-quarters. The brush still continued to be very thorny. The land to the westward appeared sandy and barren. This day they saw

_____
* An animal which burrows in the ground as a badger, and lives on grass.

8

the fires of some natives below; the number they computed at about thirty — men, women, and children. They noticed also more tracks of the woombat. On the 27th they proceeded five miles and a quarter — part of the way over another piece of clear land, without trees: they saw more native fires, and about the same number as before, but more in their direct course. From the top of the rocks they saw a large piece of land below, clear of trees, but apparently a poor reedy swamp. They met with some good timber in this day's route. The bearing of the route for the last three days has been chiefly north and north-west.

On the 28th they proceeded about five miles and three-quarters. Not being able to find water, they did not halt till five o'clock, when they took up their station on the edge of the precipice. To their great satisfaction, they discovered that what they had supposed to be sandy barren land below the mountain, was forest land, covered with good grass and with timber of an inferior quality. In the evening they contrived to get their horses down the mountain by cutting a small trench with a hoe, which kept them from slipping, where they again tasted fresh grass for the first time since they left the forest land on the other side of the mountain. They were getting into miserable condition. Water was found about two miles below the foot of the mountain. The second camp of natives moved before them about three miles. In this day's route little timber was observed fit for building.

On the 29th, having got up the horses and laden them, they began to descend the mountain at seven o'clock through a pass in the rock, about thirty feet wide, which they had discovered the day before, when the want of water put them on the alert. Part of the descent was so steep that the horses could but just keep their footing without a load, so that, for some way, the party were obliged to carry the packages themselves. A cart road might, however, easily be made by cutting a slanting trench along the side of the mountain, which is here covered with earth. This pass is, according to their computation, about twenty miles north-west, in a straight line from the point at which they ascended the summit of the mountain. They reached the foot at nine o'clock a.m., and proceeded two miles north-north-west, mostly through open meadow land, clear of trees, the grass from two to three feet high. They encamped on the bank of a fine stream of water. The natives, as observed by the smoke of their fires, moved before them as yesterday. The dogs killed a kangaroo, which was very acceptable, as the party had lived on salt meat since they caught the last. The timber seen this day appeared rotten and unfit for building.

Sunday, the 30th, they rested in their encampment. One of the party shot a kangaroo with his rifle, at a great distance across a wide valley. The climate here was found very much colder than that of the mountain or of the settlements on the east side, where no signs of frost had made its appearance when the party set out. During the night the ground was covered with a thick frost, and a leg of the kangaroo was quite frozen. From the dead and brown appearance of the grass it was evident that the weather had been severe for some time past. We were all much surprised at this degree of cold and frost in the latitude of about 34°. The track of the emu was noticed at several places near the camp.

On the Monday they proceeded about six miles, south-west and west, through

9

forest land, remarkably well watered, and several open meadows, clear of trees, and covered with high good grass. They crossed two fine streams of water. Traces of the natives presented themselves in the fires they had left the day before, and in the flowers of the honeysuckle tree scattered around, which had supplied them with food. These flowers, which are shaped like a bottle-brush, are very full of honey. The natives on this side of the mountains appear to have no huts like those on the eastern side, nor do they strip the bark or climb the trees. From the shavings and pieces of sharp stones which they had left, it was evident that they had been busily employed in sharpening their spears.

The party encamped by the side of a fine stream of water, at a short distance from a high hill, in the shape of a sugar loaf. In the afternoon they ascended its summit, from whence they descried all around, forest or grass land, sufficient in extent in their opinion, to support the stock of the colony for the next thirty years. This was the extreme point of their journey. The distance they had travelled they computed at about fifty-eight miles nearly north-west; that is, fifty miles through the mountain, (the greater part of which they had walked over three times,) and eight miles through the forest land beyond it, reckoning the descent of the mountain to be half-a mile to the foot.

The timber observed this day still appeared unfit for building. The stones at the bottom of the rivers appeared very fine, large-grained, dark colored granite, of a kind quite different from the mountain rocks, or from any stones which they had ever seen in the colony. Mr. Blaxland and one of the men nearly lost the party to-day by going too far in the pursuit of a kangaroo.

They now conceived that they had sufficiently accomplished the design of their undertaking, having surmounted all the difficulties which had hitherto prevented the interior of the country from being explored, and the colony from being extended. They had partly cleared, or, at least, marked out, a road by which the passage of the mountain might easily be effected. Their provisions were nearly expended, their clothes and shoes were in very bad condition, and the whole party were ill with bowel complaints. These considerations determined them therefore, to return home by the track they came. On Tuesday, the 1st of June, they arrived at the foot of the mountain which they had descended, where they encamped for the night. The following day they began to ascend the mountain at seven o'clock, and reached the summit at ten; they were obliged to carry the packages themselves part of the ascent. They encamped in the evening at one of their old stations. One of the men had left his great coat on the top of the rock, where they reloaded the horses, which was found by the next party who traversed the mountain. On the 3rd they reached another of their old stations. Here, during the night, they heard a confused noise arising from the eastern settlements below, which, after having been so long accustomed to the death-like stillness of the interior, had a very striking effect. On the 4th they arrived at the end of their marked track, and encamped in the forest land where they had cut the grass for their horses. One of the horses fell this day with his load, quite exhausted, and was with difficulty got on, after having his load put on the other horses. The next day, the 5th, was the most unpleasant and fatiguing they had experienced. The track not being marked, they had great difficulty in finding their way back to the river, which they did not reach till four o'clock p.m. They then once more encamped for the night to refresh themselves and the horses. They had no provisions now left except a little flour, but procured some from the settlement on the other side of the river. On Sunday, the 6th of June, they crossed the river after breakfast, and reached their homes, all in good health. The winter had not set in on this side of the mountain, nor had there been any frost.

Appendix.

Government Order.

GOVERNMENT HOUSE,
SYDNEY, FEB. 12, 1814.

IT having been long deemed an object of great importance, by His Excellency the Governor, to ascertain what resources this colony might possess in the interior, beyond its present known and circumscribed limits, with a view to meet the necessary demands of its rapidly increasing population; and the great importance of the discovery of new tracks of good soil, being much enhanced by the consideration of the long-continued droughts of the present season, so injurious in their effects to every class of the community in the colony: His Excellency was pleased, some time since, to equip a party of men, under the direction of Mr. George W. Evans, one of the Assistant Land Surveyors, (in whose zeal and abilities for such an undertaking he had well-founded reason to confide,) and to furnish him with written instructions for his guidance, in endeavoring to discover a passage over the Blue Mountains, and ascertaining the qualities and general properties of the soil he should meet with to the westward of them.

This object having been happily effected, and Mr. Evans returned with his entire party, all in good health: the Governor is pleased to direct that the following summary of his tour of discovery, extracted from his own journal, shall be published for general information: —

Mr. Evans, attended by five men, selected for their general knowledge of the country, and habituated to such difficulties as might be expected to occur, was supplied with horses, arms, and ammunition, and a plentiful store of provisions for a two months' tour. His instructions were, that he should commence the ascent of the Blue Mountains, from the extremity of the present known country at Emu Island, distant about thirty-six miles from Sydney, and thence proceed in as nearly a west direction as the nature of the country he had to explore would admit, and to continue his journey as far as his means would enable him.

On Saturday, the 20th of November last, the party proceeded from Emu Island; and on the fifth day, having then effected their passage over the Blue Mountains, arrived at the commencement of a valley on the western side of them, having passed over several tracks of tolerably good soil, but also over much rugged and very difficult mountain: proceeding through this valley, which Mr. Evans describes as beautiful and fertile, with a rapid stream running through it, he arrived at the termination of the tour lately made by Messrs. G. Blaxland, W. C. Wentworth, and Lieutenant Lawson. Continuing in the Western direction, prescribed in his instructions, for the course of twenty-one days from this station, Mr. Evans then found it necessary to return; and on the 8th of January he arrived back at Emu Island, after an excursion of seven complete weeks. During the course of this tour Mr. Evans passed over several plains of great extent, interspersed with hills and valleys, abounding in the richest soil, and with various streams of water and chains of ponds. The country he traversed measured ninety-eight miles and a half beyond the termination of Messrs. Blaxland, Wentworth, and Lawson's tour, and not less than one hundred and fifty miles from Emu Island. The greater part of these plains are described as being nearly free of timber and brushwood, and in capacity equal (in Mr. Evans's opinion) to every demand which this colony may have for an extension of tillage and pasture lands for a century to come. The stream already mentioned continues its course in a westerly direction, and for several miles, passing through the valleys, with many and great accessions of other streams becomes a capacious and beautiful river, abounding in fish of very large size and fine flavour, many of which weighed not less than fifteen pounds. This river is supposed to empty itself into the ocean, on the western side of New South Wales, at a distance of from two to three hundred miles from the termination of the tour. From the summits of some very high hills, Mr. Evans saw a vast extent of flat country, lying in a westerly direction, which appeared to be bounded at a distance of about forty miles by other hills. The general description of these hitherto unexplored regions, given by Mr. Evans, is, that they very far surpass, in beauty and fertility of soil, any he has seen in New South Wales or Van Diemen's Land.

In consideration of the importance of these discoveries, and calculating upon the effect they may have on the future prosperity of this colony, His Excellency the Governor is pleased to announce his intention of presenting Mr. Evans with a grant of one thousand acres of land in Van Diemen's Land, where he is to be stationed as Deputy Surveyor; and, further, to make him a pecuniary reward from the Colonial Funds, in acknowledgment of his diligent and active services on this occasion.

His Excellency also means to make a pecuniary reward to the two free men who accompanied Mr. Evans, and a grant of land to each of them. To the three convicts who also assisted in this excursion the Governor means to grant conditional pardons, and a small portion of land to each of them, these men having performed the services required of them entirely to the satisfaction of Mr. Evans.

The Governor is happy to embrace this opportunity of conveying his acknowledgments to Gregory Blaxland and William Charles Wentworth, Esqs., and Lieutenant William Lawson, of the Royal Veteran Company, for their enterprising and arduous exertions on the the tour of discovery which they voluntarily performed in the month of May last, when they effected a passage over the Blue Mountains, and proceeded to the extremity of the first valley, particularly alluded to in Mr. Evans's Tour, and being the first Europeans who had accomplished the passage over the Blue Mountains. The Governor, desirous to confer on these gentlemen substantial marks of his sense of their meritorious exertions on this occasion, means to present each of them with a grant of one thousand acres of land in this newly discovered country.

By command of His Excellency the Governor.

J. T. CAMPBELL,

SECRETARY.

www.ingramcontent.com/pod-product-compliance
Lightning Source LLC
Chambersburg PA
CBHW060047050426
42448CB00012B/3144